alessandra
keep Reading!

For my family...

Ushma Multani, Author

Inspired by her favorite quote, "don't just dream, do," Ushma took to writing as a way to share her journey. Having lived in India, California and Massachusetts, she recognized the value of family, cultural traditions, and community at an early age. Through this book, Ushma wants to help families build memories while sharing a piece of her own traditions.

A mother of two young children, Ushma resides in the suburbs of Boston with her husband.

Ann Gagliano, Illustrator

The human figure has always been her biggest inspiration—always moving and changing, no pose or expression ever the same. As a graduate of Parsons School of Design, she has been trained to work best with a five minute sketch, capturing gesture and attitude through unconscious line. She seeks character, not perfection.

Ann is a mother of two and resides outside Boston, Massachusetts with her husband and cute papillon, Meeko.

Reena and the Diwali Star

Written by
Ushma Multani

Illustrated by
Ann Gagliano

Boston, Massachusetts

"I'm so excited! Tomorrow is the start of Diwali and I can't wait to get my present!" Reena giggled with excitement. "What are your favorite memories from our celebration last year in Mumbai?" asked her mother.

As she fell asleep, Reena recalled the long flight to India and the wonder she felt when she got off the plane.

Reena's parents both grew up in India and her grandparents still live in Mumbai. When she spotted her grandparents waiting for her at the airport, she raced excitedly into their arms.

The first thing that caught her eye was the number of people everywhere.

Mumbai was beautiful and colorful but a bit noisy.

Lord Ganesha   Goddess Lakshmi

She saw homes, temples and buildings brightly lit up to celebrate Diwali. Diwali is the festival of lights. "On this special day we light diyas and give thanks to Lord Ganesha and Goddess Lakshmi," said Reena's Grandma.

"See this, Reena?" her grandmother cuddled her close in her arms. "This is a Diya. It is an oil lamp made from clay and we light them on Diwali to celebrate the victory of good over evil."

"Now let's talk about how we can get you a Diwali present! Do you know the story of the Diwali Star? It is a special star that can make your wish come true."

Write your wish here. ↓

"Every year, children write their wish for a Diwali present in this book." Grandma pulled out a colorful book and showed it to her.

"The Diwali Star teaches children to be kind and responsible while enjoying the festivities of Diwali," said Grandma. "For your wish to come true, you need to complete 5 Diwali activities, just like the 5 points of a star."

5.
Make a Diwali Dessert

Plant a Seed 4.

1. Make a Diwali card

2. Design a Rangoli Pattern

3. Act of Kindness

Reena wrote down her wish in the book. This wish was something very special to her and she had shared it with her parents. She was excited and started working on the 5 activities right away.

On her last day of vacation, Grandma took Reena shopping. Reena picked a beautiful lehenga and some shiny bangles. Her lehenga was a long sparkly pink skirt.

As Reena fell asleep, it was Diwali morning back in Boston....

Reena woke up to the smell of freshly made pedas.
She was excited for the Diwali celebrations to begin.

That evening, the family offered prayers and Reena recited the Gayatri Mantra. It was a short prayer that she had learned from her mother and this was how her family began Diwali celebrations every year.

Gayatri Mantra:
oṃ bhūr bhuvaḥ suvaḥ
tatsaviturvareṇyaṃ
bhargo devasyadhīmahi
dhiyo yo naḥ prachodayāt

Her mother had shared that the meaning of the prayer was a way to show appreciation and being thankful for what you have.

There were smiles everywhere when Diwali guests arrived and wished each other "Happy Diwali." Reena excitedly waited for her Diwali present, she had worked hard to complete all 5 activities and wanted her wish to come true.

She ran down the stairs and giggled with excitement as she knew her wish had come true. Reena could not have been happier.

Turn this page and learn how to make your wish come true!
Happy Diwali!

Activity #1
Make a Diwali Card

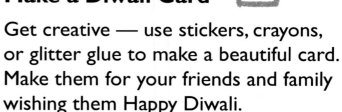

Get creative — use stickers, crayons, or glitter glue to make a beautiful card. Make them for your friends and family wishing them Happy Diwali.

Activity #2
Design a Rangoli Pattern

Rangolis are patterns made on the floor at the entrance of a house. They are created by using flowers, grains or colored powder and are a way to welcome friends and family. Make sure it is bright and sparkly!

Activity #3
Act of Kindness

Donate toys, books, clothes and/or volunteer time. A typical ritual before Diwali is to clean the house, give back, or donate items to the community.

Activity #4
Plant a Seed

A great way to show you care is to give something back to Planet Earth. It could be as simple as planting a special flower or tree.

Make a Diwali Dessert

Milk peda (pay-daa) was Reena's favorite and she enjoyed making it with her grandmother.

Milk Peda Recipe

Ingredients:

5 cups of whole milk
¼ cup regular sugar
¼ tsp green cardamom powder

Instructions:

Pour 5 cups of milk into a large pot on low/medium heat.
Bring the milk to a boil, stirring occasionally to prevent it from sticking to the bottom for about 8 minutes.
After 25 minutes, the milk will thicken to a cream.
Continue stirring over low heat. After 50 minutes, it changes into a paste.
Now add ¼ cup sugar.
Continue to keep stirring until the sugar dissolves.
Continue to cook on low heat until the mixture can hold its shape.
Now let it cool slightly, and then take the cooled mixture and form into small balls.
These balls are called milk pedas.
Serve milk peda and you can store the rest in an airtight container.

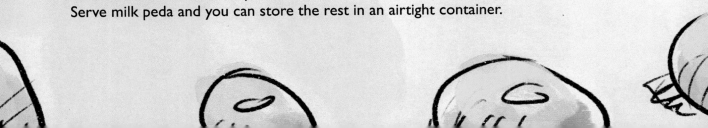

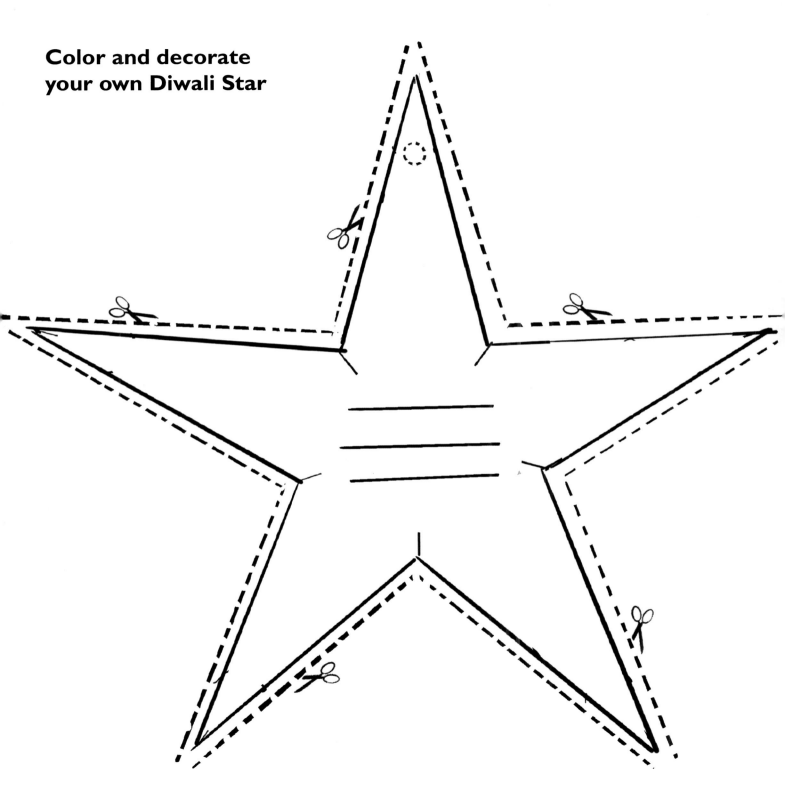

Color and decorate
your own Diwali Star

Made in the USA
Middletown, DE
29 September 2021

Reena and the Diwali Star

Absorb the culture and traditions of the Diwali festival as you learn about the Diwali Star with Reena, and find out how to use the Diwali Star to make your wish come true.

Glowing lights, colorful scenes surround Reena as she travels from Boston to Mumbai and back. On her journey, she learns about the values of kindness and responsibility, how she can give back to her community, and also enjoys making a fun new dessert.

This interactive book will give you a chance to complete activities together while making new memories. Do you think Reena's wish will come true?

ISBN 9780578969886